The Illustrated Story of President

# JOSEPH FIELDING SMITH

Great Leaders of The Church
of Jesus Christ of Latter-day Saints

The Illustrated Story of President Joseph Fielding Smith
Great Leaders of The Church of Jesus Christ
of Latter-day Saints

Copyright © 1982 by
Eagle Systems International
P.O. Box 508
Provo, Utah 84603

ISBN: 0-938762-10-9
Library of Congress Catalog Card No.: 82-71682

Fourth Printing April 1987

First Edition

Lithographed in U.S.A.
by
COMMUNITY PRESS, INC.


A Member of
The American Bookseller's Association
New York, New York

The Illustrated Story of President

# JOSEPH FIELDING SMITH

## Great Leaders of The Church
## of Jesus Christ of Latter-day Saints

We thank the family of Joseph Fielding Smith for their generous help and cooperation in this project.

AUTHOR
Della Mae Rasmussen

ILLUSTRATOR
B. Keith Christensen

DIRECTOR AND CORRELATOR
Lael J. Woodbury

ADVISORS AND EDITORS
Paul & Millie Cheesman
Mark Ray Davis
L. Norman Egan
Annette Hullinger
Beatrice W. Friel

PUBLISHER
Steven R. Shallenberger

# A
# Biography Of
# JOSEPH FIELDING SMITH

One of the most devoted and diligent leaders the Church has ever had was born in Salt Lake City, Utah, on July 19, 1876. He was given the name of his father, Joseph Fielding Smith, who was a member of the Council of the Twelve Apostles. His mother was Julina Lambson Smith.

Joseph Fielding grew up in a large and happy family. He learned to work hard helping his family, and he gained a strong testimony of the truthfulness of the gospel of Jesus Christ. He was a very intelligent young boy and diligently studied both his schoolwork and the scriptures at a very early age.

Joseph Fielding Smith married Louie E. Shurtliff in the Salt Lake Temple in 1898 and not long afterward, at the age of twenty-two, he was called to serve a mission for the Church in the British Isles. Upon his return home after a worthy mission he obtained work in the Church Historian's Office. He was immediately called to responsible Church positions, and in 1908 he was appointed director and librarian of the Genealogical Society. His wife, Louie, died in 1908. He then married Ethel G. Reynolds. Louie and Joseph Fielding had two daughters, and his wife Ethel had nine children. President Smith was always a kind and loving father to his children. He taught them to love the Lord and the gospel of Jesus Christ.

Joseph Fielding's wife, Ethel, died in 1937, and he later married Jessie Ella Evans.

President Smith traveled worldwide in his Church assignments. He was an outstanding gospel scholar and wrote a great number of books and pamphlets to help people understand the gospel. He also gave many talks calling the Saints to repent of their sins and to live righteously.

At the age of eighty-nine Joseph Fielding was named a counselor in the First Presidency.

Joseph Fielding Smith appeared uncommonly healthy and youthful, even at an advanced age. One thing he particularly liked in his later life was flying in military jets with the Utah National Guard. He became an honorary officer in that organization.

Joseph Fielding Smith was sustained as President of The Church of Jesus Christ of Latter-day Saints on January 23, 1970. He was ninety-three years of age, the oldest man to fill that position. He was the only son of a President of the Church to also become President. His years as President of the Church are thought by many to be among the most progressive of Church history. He was actively involved in both his family activities and his calling as prophet, seer, and revelator until the day he died of a heart attack while sitting quietly in his home on July 2, 1972, at the age of ninety-five.

If someone had said, "We've waited a long, long time for you, young man!" to the baby son born to Joseph F. and Julina Smith on a hot summer day, July 19, 1876, in Salt Lake City, Utah, they would have been correct. The parents had been waiting and praying for ten years! It was not that they had no children at all. Joseph F. and his first wife, Julina, did have three beautiful daughters, but they wanted a son to carry the respected name of his father, Joseph Fielding Smith. The baby did indeed have a noble heritage. His great-uncle was the Prophet Joseph Smith, his grandfather was Hyrum Smith, and his father was an apostle of the Lord.

Little Joseph Fielding was actually the tenth child in his father's family. Joseph F. Smith's wives and their children lived together at the time in a large home in downtown Salt Lake City. The house was bursting with children and with happiness. Apostle Joseph F. Smith welcomed each of his children as a special spirit sent by Heavenly Father. He welcomed many of them, too, since there were eventually forty-five children in his own family. They added three adopted children to their family, making forty-eight children in all. Imagine living in a family with four dozen children! There was much love and security among them, as each thought of the others as full brothers and sisters. There was always someone to play and work with, and they defended each other in any difficulty.

The Smith family's biggest worry was that the government would not allow them

to live peacefully. Federal marshals were trying to break up the multiple families in the Church and from time to time would tramp through the Smith house searching for the father. President Joseph F. Smith sometimes had to hide to escape from them, and during part of Joseph Fielding's early years he did not see his father very often. When President Smith could come home, he spent the time teaching his children the principles of the gospel. Young Joseph Fielding admired his father and often thought to himself, "He is the best, finest, and wisest man in the whole world!"

As soon as Joseph Fielding Smith grew big enough, he joined his brothers and sisters in doing farm and household chores. He irrigated and went "haying" with the boys and men. He herded cows near the Jordan River. Sometimes he took a short "vacation" from his task and went swimming in the river!

10

Like other young boys, Joseph Fielding did not always make perfect decisions! Once at the end of a long day he and his brother Hyrum were preparing to bring in the last load of hay, the "pay-the-tithing" load, to the tithing yard.

"If we can load this last wagon up high enough, we won't have to come for another load," the boys reasoned together. So they piled the hay higher and higher. Finally they had a load of hay about twice as high as usual. Joseph Fielding rode on the top. When they took the load through the gate to the tithing yard, the bar across the top of the gate knocked Joseph Fielding off and he fell to the ground and broke his leg. It was a hard way to learn an important lesson!

The work was not all out in the fields either. Joseph Fielding and his brothers and sisters took care of a large garden, where they grew peas, beans, turnips, and other vegetables. They also took care of a flock of chickens, three milk cows, and a few horses.

12

Of course, it was not all work. They had fun and played games, too. In the early summer evenings, someone would call, "Come on, let's play hide-and-seek!" Quickly an eager group of children would gather from all directions. One of Joseph Fielding's favorite hiding places was a secret spot among the fruit trees and grapevines. From there he could run out and usually "come in free."

Sometimes children today like to surprise their parents by doing grown-up things, like fixing breakfast before mother gets up in the morning. Joseph Fielding was no different. One day he thought to himself, "I will surprise Mama and show her that I can milk the cow." So he secretly milked the cow to prove that he could do it. He did such a good job and his mother was so pleased that she said, "I did not realize that you were able to milk the cow all by yourself! You may take over the job now, Joseph." Perhaps it was Joseph Fielding's turn to be surprised. Anyway, the job became his to do!

Joseph had another important responsibility. When he was ten years old, his mother asked him to be the stable boy and buggy driver for her. She was a midwife and helped other mothers when they gave birth to new babies, as there were no hospitals there. At any time of the day or night when his mother was called out to help, Joseph hitched up the horse, "Old Meg," and drove his mother to the home where the baby was to be born. It seemed to Joseph that this happened mostly on cold, dark, stormy winter nights. He often had to make their way over muddy, rough roads and then wait for hours for his mother. Once in a while he must have thought, "How is it that so many babies are born in the middle of the night, especially cold winter nights. I wish all babies would be born on warm, sunny summer days!"

Besides Old Meg, Joseph Fielding had some adventures with a family horse named "Junie." The boy was instructed to keep Junie locked in the barn, but Junie would simply take the strap on the door of her stall between her teeth and lift it over the top of the post. Then off she would trot into the yard. She never ran away; she would just walk nonchalantly through the garden, tramping right on the vegetables! This exasperated Joseph Fielding. "That Junie!" he would say. "What shall I do with her? She is almost as smart as a person!"

Junie had still another trick. Whenever she got out into the yard, she would turn on the water tap that was used to fill the water trough for the other animals. Sometimes even in the middle of the night Joseph would hear the water running in the water trough. He would think wearily, "Well, I have to get up and turn off the water and get Junie back in the barn." It was hard to get up in the dark and go tend to Junie, but Joseph always did it.

Joseph's father scolded him a bit: "Son, can't you keep Junie in the barn? Sometimes that horse seems smarter than you are! I guess I'll just have to show you how to lock her in so she can't get out."

Joseph's father took the strap and, instead of throwing it over the top of the post, he buckled it around the post and under a crossbar. He said to Junie, "Young lady, let's see you get out of there now!" Joseph and his father walked back toward the house, but before they got there, Junie came trotting up behind them. Joseph Fielding could not help laughing. "Father," he teased, "do you think that Junie could be smarter than you, too?"

Young Joseph looked forward to certain days. One, of course, was Christmas. Why, he might even receive as much as a book, an orange, and a few nuts! But perhaps even better were Thanksgiving Day and the celebrations on the fourth and twenty-fourth of July. These were the days when the family had ice cream! As he ate the cool, sweet confection, he wondered, "Could anything, ever, anywhere, taste as good as this?"

Joseph Fielding proved to be a superior student, both at home and school. He received a Book of Mormon from his father when he was eight years old. By the time he was ten, he had read it through twice. He would hurry with his chores so as to climb up in the hayloft to read the book. Other times, instead of playing with the other children, he would sit in the shade of a tree and study his scriptures.

It became clear that he had a strong spiritual nature. He especially liked watching the workmen as they built the Salt Lake Temple not far from his home. He saw the wagons hauling the huge granite stones from Little Cottonwood Canyon. But the work moved slowly, and sometimes he wondered, "Will I live long enough to see the temple finished?" He did, of course, and was even able to go to the first dedication on April 6, 1893. He was almost seventeen years old, and he always remembered the event as a highlight in his life.

23

When Joseph Fielding was nineteen years old, he asked to have his patriarchal blessing. From this remarkable blessing he learned that "much is expected of you . . . you will live to a good old age . . . it is the will of the Lord that you shall become a mighty man in Zion . . . you will sit in counsel with your brethren and preside among the people. . . . You will travel much at home and abroad, by land and water, laboring in the ministry . . . no power shall prevail against you." He was also blessed with wisdom and the promise that God would preserve his body until he had completed all he had been sent to earth to do. Joseph Fielding Smith was to be one of the Lord's chosen servants and would hold high offices in the Church.

As Joseph grew from boyhood to manhood, he studied at the Latter-day Saint College, but he also continued to help his family with every type of chore. Sometimes he would mix a large batch of bread at night, then get up early to put it in pans for baking before leaving for his job at Zion's Cooperative Mercantile Institution. At ZCMI he put in long hours. In describing his job he said, "I worked like a workhorse all day long and was tired out when night came, carrying sacks of flour and sugar and hams and bacons on my back. I weighed 150 pounds and often had to carry 200-pound sacks on my shoulders." He continued, "I was a very foolish fellow because ever since that time my shoulders have been just a little out of kilter . . . !" Joseph Fielding was never afraid of work!

Joseph grew up to be an uncommonly handsome young man and in the year 1894 a significant event occurred in his life. A young woman came to attend school in Salt Lake City. She lived with the Smith family. Her name was Louie Shurtliff, and as soon as Joseph Fielding met her, he wished he had the courage to say, "You are the most beautiful girl I have ever seen." He courted Louie for the next three years, and after she graduated from the university, Joseph and Louie were married for time and eternity in the Salt Lake Temple on April 26, 1898.

He had always planned to fulfill a mission, so the couple was not surprised when less than a year after their marriage Joseph received a mission call to Great Britain. It was difficult to leave his beautiful young wife, but he thought of the hymn, "I'll Go Where You Want Me To Go, Dear Lord," and he went!

He and Louie were lonely for each other, but Joseph wrote, ". . . I know that our happiness is dependent upon my faithfulness while I am here." Another time he wrote, "I would rather stay here forever than come home without an honorable record and release, for I should never be happy and would make you and our parents miserable." Joseph served a worthy mission and was released in June, 1901.

Joseph returned home to a glad reunion with his wife and other members of his family. He took a position in the Church Historian's Office and immediately became involved in Church positions of great responsibility. During the next few years he was a Sunday School teacher, a member of the general board for the Young Men's Mutual Improvement Association, and a stake high councilman, to name only a few. There was never a young man more devoted to the affairs of the Lord.

---

THINK ABOUT IT:

1. What were some of the things that Joseph Fielding Smith learned to do as a young boy that prepared him to be a great leader in the Church?
2. What were some of the interesting experiences of his childhood?
3. Why did Joseph Fielding Smith feel it was so important that he fulfill a worthy mission?

Joseph Fielding was an unofficial secretary to his father, who had become President of the Church in October, 1901. He performed many services for his father. At one time President Joseph F. Smith became ill and sent his son Joseph Fielding to dedicate a meetinghouse. The stake authorities came with wide smiles to meet their illustrious visitor, but instead of President Joseph F. Smith, the son of the prophet stepped off the train. "I could have cried," said the stake president. "We were expecting the President of the Church and we got a boy instead!" Joseph Fielding had a fine sense of humor, so he did not take offense. In fact, he would always chuckle whenever he thought of this experience.

Joseph and his wife Louie were very happy. They were blessed with two little daughters, Josephine and Julina, and they were able to build their "dream home" in Salt Lake City. But, sadly, Louie became very ill as she was to have another child and, after much pain and suffering, she died in March, 1908. Joseph was heartbroken and tried to be both mother and father to his little girls. He thought he would never marry again. But when his father and his father-in-law heard his children crying for their mama, they said to him, "Joseph, you have got to find a mother for those little girls."

A few months later he married Ethel Georgina Reynolds, and the Smiths were a family once again. Eventually Ethel and Joseph had nine children of their own, and with Julina and Josephine, they were a family of considerable size and much happiness.

In April, 1910, there was a vacancy in the Council of the Twelve Apostles. The Brethren met and discussed the matter but could come to no decision. President Joseph F. Smith left the meeting and went alone to pray for guidance. When he returned, he stood still for a moment before saying to the other Brethren, "I feel inspired to sustain my son Joseph Fielding Smith to the position. Would you be willing to consider this appointment?" President Smith had hesitated because his son Hyrum was already a member of the Council of Twelve Apostles and another son, David, was a counselor in the Presiding Bishopric. President Smith thought Church members might criticize his choice of another son as a General Authority. Still, he had felt the inspiration of the Lord. The other Brethren immediately agreed with the choice, and Joseph Fielding Smith was sustained by them as an apostle of the Lord. Joseph Fielding himself was startled to hear his name read as the new apostle while sitting in general conference on April 6, 1910. After the meeting he hurried to tell Ethel and the children about his appointment. He announced, "I guess we'll have to sell the cow. I haven't time to take care of her anymore!"

Joseph Fielding was humble in accepting his calling, and that day began over sixty years of faithful and outstanding service to the Church as a General Authority.

He traveled widely in his duties as an apostle. He also began to write books and articles to answer gospel questions and to help the Saints live better lives. As an author he has had great and lasting influence on the Church and its members. He spoke up and taught boldly the principle of repentance and called upon every Church member to live righteously. Some people thought him stern and distant, but in reality he was a kind and loving man, who only wanted the Saints to live the gospel fully and serve the Lord.

Although he traveled a great deal, he made certain he spent many delightful hours with his children. They liked to have him tell stories about his travels as they sat at the dinner table. It was an exciting time, too, when he would say, "Let's take a lunch and a freezer of Mama's special homemade ice cream and go up the canyon for a picnic!"

Another day of fun for the Smith family came when President Smith tied an apron around his waist and began to bake pies! He made apple, peach, cherry, pumpkin, and his own recipe of mincemeat. What a treat for his boys and girls!

35

When a child was ill, President Smith walked the floor, giving the little one constant attention, nursing him or her throughout the night. He would often read, dance, or play music to help a sick child feel better. His wife Ethel said, "The man I know is a kind, loving husband and father, whose greatest ambition in life is to make his family happy, entirely forgetful of self in his efforts to do this."

It is clear that Joseph Fielding was a man of tremendous and varied talents, for besides all of this he was also a fine athlete. He always encouraged his children to be active in sports. He himself was an outstanding swimmer and a handball player who could win a game of handball from any of his sons. He did not quit playing handball until in his fifties, when his doctor insisted that he do so. Even at that age he could still win games from men ten or more years younger. He obeyed his doctor's order with regret! He enjoyed watching almost any sport, including basketball, football, and baseball, especially if his children were playing on a team.

All too soon Joseph Fielding was again to lose his choice companion. The family was greatly saddened when its wife and mother, Ethel, died in August, 1937.

Once again Joseph and his family needed a mother and wife to care for them. On April 12, 1938, he married Jessie Ella Evans, a well-known singer. She was a jolly, happy person, and she added a measure of lightheartedness to Joseph's life. They traveled together from the beginning of their marriage. Often at meetings and conferences they each spoke and then sang a duet to the delight of the Saints in many parts of the world.

They enjoyed a good joke together, too, and hung a plaque on their kitchen wall which read, "Opinions expressed by the husband in this household are not necessarily those of the management."

President Smith always seemed younger than his years. No matter how many years he lived, he always seemed to have a youthful and adventurous outlook. He began to fly in fighter jets at an age when many men want to keep their feet solidly on the ground! Joseph Fielding was invited to ride in a jet with General Alma G. Winn of the Utah National Guard and found that he liked it immensely! Sometimes he took over the plane's controls. Once Jessie took a ride with Joseph and the general and saw her husband flying the plane. "You're not going to let him fly it, are you?" she asked General Winn. "Why not," he answered. "He's done it before!"

This flying was a great delight to President Smith. On one trip in the jet he said, "It is a wonderful experience to travel in such a plane at about 500 miles per hour. We can see in all directions, into Idaho, Wyoming, Nevada, and as far away as lower Utah or beyond. It is a wonderful sight!" He was even named an honorary brigadier general in the guard and had his own uniform!

President Smith and Jessie were traveling in Europe visiting the missions of the Church at the outbreak of World War II. They went to help the missions and ended by directing an emergency operation to evacuate the missionaries from Europe. Joseph Fielding yearned to help the Saints living in Europe. He said, "My heart was sick every time we held a meeting and shook hands with the people . . . they all greeted us warmly and their friendship meant more to me than they perhaps realized. Some of them shed tears and said they were expecting grave trouble and that we would never meet again in this life. I feel sorry for them now and pray each day that the Lord will protect them through this dreadful time." President Smith and Jessie arrived home safely November 12, 1939.

Later, after the United States entered the war, Joseph Fielding's own son Lewis was killed in the service of his country. He was killed while traveling on assignment in an airplane that exploded in midair. President Smith was stunned by this tragedy and wrote, "We feel sure Lewis has some mission and has been taken by divine command. He was clean and worthy in every respect and entitled to every blessing that can be obtained. . . ." Joseph Fielding Smith took just pride in the fact that all five of his sons served missions, either before or after World War II, and that all ten of his living children were married in the temple.

Joseph Fielding Smith became President of the Twelve Apostles in April, 1951, and served faithfully in that position for nearly twenty years. He and Jessie visited almost every corner of the earth, and he loved the Saints everywhere. In August, 1955, he was visiting in Korea, where he dedicated the land to the preaching of the gospel. After the meeting he saw a young boy standing close to him with *The Children's Friend* in his hand. There was a story about Joseph Fielding Smith in it. The young boy showed President Smith the magazine and said, "See, I can read all about you now, and you ordained me a deacon last night, and now I can help with the gospel." Elder Smith put his arms around the boy with tears in his eyes. He said, "I thank the Lord for the privilege of being in this land with these marvelous people."

When Joseph Fielding was eighty-nine years old, the President of the Church, David O. McKay, appointed him a counselor in the First Presidency. On January 23, 1970, at the death of President McKay, Joseph Fielding Smith was sustained President of The Church of Jesus Christ of Latter-day Saints. He was ninety-three years old! Some people thought, "Surely he is too old to lead the Church." However, the Lord called him as the president and prophet and, as one friend said, "The Lord never makes a mistake."

President Smith's message to the people was to love God, his Son, and each other. He was president for just two and one half years, but they were vigorous years of growth and change for the Church. He traveled to all parts of the world to visit, counsel, and sustain the Saints. He continued his writing, he met with his Brethren, and he made many important decisions. People were amazed at the activity, energy, and insight of their prophet.

Still, he never neglected his beloved family. After he lost his dear wife Jessie in death on August 3, 1971, he continued to meet in family home evenings with his children and grandchildren. He was greatly blessed in health, as his eyes, ears, and mind were good, even at age ninety-five, just as he had been promised in his patriarchal blessing. He never lost his rich sense of humor. Modest and humble, as always, he continued strongly to preach repentance and rightous living. He constantly reminded the Saints that, "Wickedness never was happiness."

THINK ABOUT IT:

1. How was Joseph Fielding Smith chosen to be an apostle of the Lord?
2. In what ways was President Smith's patriarchal blessing fulfilled?
3. What special qualities did Joseph Fielding Smith possess that brought him great respect from others?

This great president and prophet died on July 2, 1972, just a few days before his ninety-sixth birthday. Apparently he simply went to sleep in his favorite chair. This was also a literal fulfillment of his patriarchal blessing and the scripture, "Those that die in me shall not taste of death." (D&C 42:46).

The life of President Joseph Fielding Smith covered almost one hundred years, from the covered wagon to the jet plane, and he loved being part of it all.

Few in the Church have been more faithful as followers of Jesus Christ. Nor has there been a greater scriptural scholar or a prophet who worked more diligently for the perfection of the Saints. He will always be remembered with love and admiration by the members of the Church that he cared for and served so well.

# TESTIMONY

My beloved Brethren and Sisters, I stand before you today, in humility and in thanksgiving, grateful for the blessings which the Lord has poured out upon me and upon my family, and upon you, the members of the Church, and all good people.

I desire to say that no man of himself can lead this Church. It is the Church of Jesus Christ—he is at the head. The Church bears his name. It has his priesthood, ministers his gospel, preaches his doctrine, and accomplishes his work.

He chooses men and calls them to be instruments in his hands to accomplish these purposes; and he guides and directs them in their labors. But men are only instruments in the Lord's hands, and the honor and glory for all that his servants accomplish is and should be ascribed unto him forever. If this were the work of man, it would fail. But it is the work of the Lord, and he does not fail. I rejoice in the work of the Lord and glory in the sure knowledge I have in my soul of its truth and divinity. With all my heart I bear witness that Jesus Christ is the Son of the living God, that he called the prophet Joseph Smith to stand at the head of this dispensation and to organize again on earth the Church and kingdom of God, and that the work in which we are engaged is true. Let us be faithful and humble. Let us live the religion of Jesus Christ, put away the weaknesses of the flesh, and cleave to the Lord and his truth with undivided hearts, with full determination to fight the good fight of faith and continue steadfast to the end, which may God grant us power to do is my prayer in the name of Jesus Christ. Amen.